PR for PENNIES

Low-cost library Public Relations

PR for PENNIES

Low-cost library Public Relations

Virginia Van Wynen Baeckler

SOURCES
Hopewell, New Jersey

Library of Congress Catalog Card Number: 77-90578
Printed in the United States of America

PR for Pennies is published by
SOURCES, 26 Hart Avenue, Hopewell, NJ 08525

You may order copies prepaid for $4.00 each by
writing to the publisher.

CONTENTS

If I could tell you what can
never be said. Listen. I
have birds in my head,
stars in my feet, clouds
on my mind!

To be Alive!

1. PUBLIC RELATIONS: What's it all about?

Public relations for non profit organizations is *not* the same as public relations in the commercial world. We do not sell what *is*, but what might be. We sell what will be true if materials are used and institutions serve. The sky is the limit. Small libraries have the same dream as large ones. Numbers mean nothing. The challenge, the hope, the joy and excitement of connecting people with knowledge is the "product" we sell. Residents of Sarah Springs, New Jersey (pop. 350) have the same chance for success as residents of Greggville, West Virginia (pop. 65). Residents of New York City have the same chance as residents of Williams Beach, Florida (pop. 1937). It is a great dream. An extraordinary dream. And now is the time to sell it.

Few insiders question the need for libraries to have quality public relations programs, but most are quick to point out that such programs cost considerable money. It is unfortunate, at this time of severe budget cutbacks, that the concepts of need and expense have so totally intertwined. Large moneyed systems readily hire commercial advertising agencies and recruit public relations staff members. Small libraries are discouraged from discovering that they can do the basics themselves with very, very few dollars.

The goal of this manual is to demystify a number of practical public relations techniques for those who wish to start producing materials on their own with a minimum of time and money. Specific focus will be concentrated on offset printing, exhibits, posters and personal speaking appearances, but readers will find that many of the principles apply to newswriting, radio and t.v. work. It is assumed that those studying this book already have a worthy message, service philosophy or program schedule to "sell," and are prepared to surrender the alibi, "But *I* can't do *that!*"

2. THE LIBRARY STEREOTYPE

Although there are delightful exceptions, the general library image is not a good one. To Joe Library Non-user, the institution is dominated by visual and accoustical negatives. Experience has taught him that libraries are quiet, frustrating, grey traps which frequently reject people, ideas, differences, trouble. The image is vividly summarized in an informal paper by Jude Burkhauser entitled, *Beware of Librarian:* Some Self Evaluative questions for Library Users.

1. When you are in a large supermarket and cannot find an item, are you ashamed (or afraid) to ask for help?

2. Do you apologize to your bank teller for "bothering" her when you approach to transact some business?

3. Do you read your own water and gas and electric meters and make monthly reports because you feel it isn't the company's job?

4. When you call a florist and order a special bouquet, do you worry if it will be too much trouble?

5. When you visit a doctor and pay him to check your heart, does he give you the stethoscope and ask you to do it yourself?

It is not simply the view of selected dissidents that libraries are such difficult, dreary places. The stereotype is so pervasive that national television advertisements use libraries as the most unlikely, unimagineable location to posit an automobile, and the most likely situation to have a sedate, bespectacled, beseated female recommending *gentle* (why not effective? or dynamic?) laxatives.*

---

* A review of several winning advertisements may be found in SLJ, Nov. 1976, p. 39.

Nor is the stereotype without basis in absolute fact! Libraries often used to be like that. Many still are today. Horror stories abound on library disservice, sometimes reaching the pages of such national forums as the *New York Times.** In polling hundreds of librarians recently for a word which epitomized the non-user's image of the library, *cold, confusing* and *bureaucratic* were the overwhelming favorites.†

In view of this, one must ask what the material which chances to reach beyond the library's walls does to dispel this dismal image? Frankly, very little. The wordy flyers and formal book lists so common to the library world, reinforce the notion that libraries are stereotyped quite correctly. Let's take a moment and consider the following brochure, which was printed for general distribution with the unstated purpose of "attracting new users to the library."**

---

* NYT, October 17, 1976, p. NJ 33.

† Others high on the frequency list include: impersonal, elitist, old fashioned, unfriendly, intimidating, forbidding, stuffy, boring, quiet, imposing, condescending.

** The name, address and certain identifiable details have been changed for publication. The graphic and content materials remain essentially unaltered.

LEWIS LIBRARY

Welcome to the Lewis Library.

Your registration at the library provides you entry to a world of fact, pleasure and knowledge. The trained staff and professionals will provide assistance and guidance in the use of our materials and will inform you of the many special programs held at the library.

Use your card frequently to discover the wide range of things available to patrons.

Responsibility

Each borrower is responsible for items circulated on his library card and all fines accruing on same. No one should lend his card to anyone else for any reason.

If it is necessary, books may be returned by depository when the library is closed. Records must never be returned in the depository.

Books will not be issued without presentation of library card. Be sure to keep your card in a safe place and present only when charging books out.

Lost cards may only be replaced 36 hours after re-registration and payment of a 50 cent lost card fee. An additional payment is made for repeated loss of card.

Registrations

Resident	No Fee
Non-resident adult	$10.00 per year
Non-resident child	$5.00 per year

Borrowing Privileges

> 10 books per card (limit of 3 from 1 week section)
> 6 record albums per adult card
> 2 cassettes per adult card
> 2 framed art reproductions per adult card
> Books will be inter - library loaned and reserved
> at the librarian's discretion

Renewals

> Library materials cannot be renewed on borrower's card or transferred to an associate card. No exceptions.

Postal Reserves

> 13 cents will be charged for any book in the collection. Limit: 4 at a time.

Loan Period

General	4 weeks
Records	2 weeks
Tapes	2 weeks
New Fiction	1 week
Art works	3 weeks

Fines

> Overdue books are subject to a fine of 5 cents per day on 4 week books. A fine of 10 cents per day will be charged on recordings, tapes, and 1 week books. Sundays and holidays are included.

> Art works are subject to a fine of 50 cents per day.

> 15 cents is charged for a lost date card.

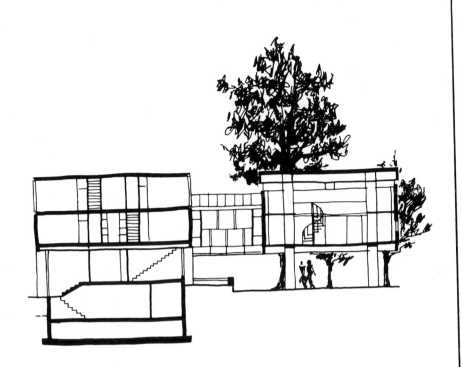

LIBRARY HOURS

Monday through Thursday	10:00 A. M. - 8:30 P. M.
Friday and Saturday	10:00 A. M. - 8:30 P. M.

SUMMER HOURS

Monday and Thursday	10:00 A. M. - 8:30 P. M.
Tuesday, Wednesday, Friday, and Saturday	10:00 A. M. - 4:30 P. M.

First impressions are critical, since most people will not devote more than a glance to library brochures. In this case, a quick perusal yields the following criticisms: the flyer tells people exactly what they already know, it speaks in stiff library jargonese, it is *not* inviting in the least, and it in no way deviates from the national stereotype. The casual reader will presume (correctly or not) that this is simply one more tired library.

If we are to learn from this well meaning but mediocre public relations attempt, we should go back and go over each page in detail.

The original brochure was printed on legal sized, grey textured paper in navy ink. As a thrifty taxpayer, dollar signs flash and I assume that there must be an important message to warrant such expense; oversized paper costs extra, colored paper costs extra, texture costs extra, colored ink costs extra. And whatever the cost, why grey and navy? Good libraries are anything but grey inside, and that fact should be radiated with corresponding joyous color.

Obviously the cover is dominated by a picture. Note in particular the age, dress and facial expressions of the people, keeping in mind that this is trying to *attract new folks to the library*. Unfortunately, this seems to typify the matronly, female library reader with purse, hat and henpecked hubby in hand. Poor male-person, with frowning face, tie and diminutive size, invites a sensitive human's pity as he is dragged, unwilling, to the library.

Where is the life? Where is the action? The children? The Blacks and minorities? What would happen if I took my kids to this library, sat on the floor, and read too loudly about wiggysnoops? Census figures for 1970 show that this community has a minority population of 21%, and a median age of 23.8. It would seem that the drawing might all too accurately reflect the *actual* library user and *not* the world that exists "out there" . . . that the library purports to be inviting inside.

Placed invisibly within the drawing is the sales pitch for the institution: (we have) a well balanced collection. Really! What miserable library jargonese. Most people want the book which they ask for *now*. Balance is not a readily recognized virtue in their minds. What *is* appealing is that librarians will go to any length to get the book which is needed. No library is big enough to satisfy everyone on the spot. But a few hops in the interlibrary network will bring reward for almost every request. *This* is something to sell.

The opening words of page one sound an ominous formal note. Subsequent lines confirm and reconfirm this attitude. Consider the phrases: your registration . . . provides you entry . . . the trained staff and professionals . . . will provide assistance . . . will inform you. It is shocking to see a library consider its wealth so possessively: "our" materials. Then too, there is the awesome imperative, "Use your card often," as if to say, "or else."

Out wriggles an accusing finger and points directly at the public: RESPONSIBILITIES. Don't do this, you must not do that, be careful, be careful, be careful. This highly negative mumbo-jumbo sounds familiar. *Very* familiar. One can almost see Miss Picklepuss scowling at patrons and pronouncing the rules. Everyone knows that the library customer is always guilty.

We have now covered one half of the Lewis Library brochure. We have not discovered anything inviting. The cover is hopeless. The verbiage is stiff and negative. As we continue we must look for something to quickly and dramatically contradict the general picture which has emerged.

Help is not on the way. One reads the opening title on page two and is severely offended: BORROWING PRIVILEGES. Has it not occurred to this library that people pay good money for these materials and services? They might prefer to think of their taxes as providing them with their rightful due. One wonders also, why the librarian's *discretion* must enter into the question of which book a patron desires to reserve.

Read carefully the section of RENEWALS. Is it possible? A library which cannot, under any circumstances, renew a book? Surely, this can't be true.

FINES! The accusing finger points again. If you don't live up to your privileges and responsibilities, the establishment has a weapon to torture you with. Ugly, simply ugly.

Consider what has been covered. Certainly nothing new. Certainly nothing inviting. There is not a single item which pleasantly states what is unique about this library, what it *really* believes and *loves*. Absolutely nothing reveals a jig or jag difference from the intolerable grey image of "the library." No one will argue that there is a place for clearly stated fine schedules (if one believes in fines) and such details. But these facts could easily be printed on an attractive half-sheet at one third the cost. There is nothing appealing about being fined, and it is not a rational line of attack in a brochure designed to attract attention and lure new customers.

Libraries have coasted too long with this sort of unthinking prose and infantile graphics. We have been the nice guys, the sweet ladies, who do things the way they've always been done, don't say much, and don't know anything about modern typewriters and advertising theory. But it's time to learn. Time to catch up to the Madison Avenue made world in which we live. Time to zap the library stereotype before it permanently zaps us.

3. THINK BEFORE YOU INK: words, ideas, pictures

When institutions place their names and a litter of words on paper, they have entered into the world of advertising. Certainly it is much easier to conceive of that fine schedule, reading list, children's story hour announcement as a simple "in house" memo, for to imagine it in competition with Coca Cola and Mac Donald's is ludicrous. But in fact, advertising it is. And if it is to have the slightest impact, it must be done very well. Barton-Gillett, a leading firm in the field of institutional communications, has expressed the battle for attention in these words:

> . . . anyone with a message worth hearing — one aimed at penetrating the receiver's attention and stimulating a response passional as well as cerebral — battles great apathy; not a quiet, peaceful apathy, but one constructed of microphones and cameras, jingles and bumper stickers, paper and paint, handshakes and phonograph records, department store decorations and movie marquees, and a myriad of separate, compartmented relationships with other human beings. There is so much going on that is exciting — or at least superficially stimulating — that the wavelengths are full of static.*

Looking at the problem from another angle, Charles Schultz has estimated that he has 16 seconds in which to present Charlie Brown's message graphically and verbally. The National Alliance for Business recommends that its PR people be prepared to explain the operations of the NAB in 30 seconds.†

---

* *Speaking to the Wind,* The Barton-Gillet Company, New York, pp.(5-6).

† *Pointers for Publicists,* p. 9. NAB, Public Affairs Department, Washington, D.C.

For libraries to effectively compete in the marketplace, they must present their message with exceptional quality, brevity and brilliance. To do this without advertising agency help is not as difficult as it might seem.

Every person involved with library public relations, whether or not he is actually the person to design and produce materials, should have at his fingertips a file of advertisements that he has liked. After all, who is a better guinea pig than the busy administrator/librarian? If an ad has caught the eye, it probably has caught countless others. It probably represents a fat account at an outstanding ad agency. Why not capitalize on someone else's monetary investment?

Let's take some examples of what might be in an idea file. In 1970 the Congressional Information Service distributed packets of free posters to public libraries. The subject — Federal documents — sounds pedantic, but the execution was dazzling. For example:

Does sex make a difference?

Sexploitation is but one form of job discrimination. Race, religion, and ethnic background are also factors. So is age.

Just how serious are these problems, and what is the outlook for positive change?

Ask your librarian.

If you have a question of fact, there's a good chance that some agency of the U.S. Government has already published the answer, and that you can easily find it in your library's collection of Federal documents.

What the Government knows, you can know. All you have to do is ask!

The shock appeal of the "line", reinforced by the graphic, evokes a smile of astonishment. What? Is this for real? What's the idea? And most readers will get into the real message. Outstanding! Imagine a library posting this at the front door. Or better yet, at the reference desk with a voluptuous young librarian. Into the idea file it goes.

Frequently magazine advertising should be clipped for its condensed working sequences. Simple and direct, the words can easily be adapted for future library use. Eastern Airlines and Holiday Inn have: "Inviting. Our islands. Our prices." Why not transpose this to: Inviting. Our people. Our service. The U.S. Virgin Islands Division of Tourism advertises brightly under the banner: "What a life!" Consider: What a library!

Think not that everything in the "file" need fit neatly. Next in line might be a life sized bikinied beauty recommending Coppertone or travel to Jamaica. The possibilities for life sized figures are boundless, but these particular lovelies make extraordinary sense when combined with the above mentioned poster for government documents. Imagine walking by Lewis Library and seeing such a display! It would turn our first impression around and immediately catapult us through the door.

There are many expensive, powerful ideas and words on television.* When a good ad line goes by, write it down immediately and meditate upon how to modify the message or syntax for library use. One evening of boob tubing should supply enough inspiration for a year. Take Chevrolet's: "Created to be elegant." It could become: Lewis Library. Created to Serve. Or, Created to serve . . . you! Or, Created to share. Or, Created by people, to serve people. Numerous other possibilities come to mind at the stimulus of Chevrolet's four carefully selected words. Be certain to scribble down "creations" at the moment they occur and transfer them to your growing idea file as soon as possible. Many great ideas are buried in busy minds, never to surface again!

Take a moment now and try your hand at this television thievery on the following Advertising Worksheet. Space is generous for instant inspirations to be written down.

---

* For a revealing look at the monumental budgets of TV's 60 second commercials, see New York Magazine, March 28, 1977, pp. 42-5.

ADVERTISING WORKSHEET

HAVE IT YOUR WAY. (Burger King)

THERE'S JUST ONE WORD FOR IT. (Schlitz)

WE'RE WORKING HARDER TO SERVE YOU BETTER. (Con Edison)

WE WANT TO HELP YOU DO THINGS RIGHT. (Stanley)

SHARING. THAT'S THE HEART OF THE MATTER. (Chevron)

TOUGH TESTING MAKES TOUGH CARS. (Ford)

SEARS. WHERE AMERICA SHOPS.

CREATED TO BE ELEGANT. (Chevrolet)

I'M A LIPTON TEA LOVER.

THE SYSTEM IS THE SOLUTION. (Bell Telephone)

I ASKED FOR IT. I GOT IT. (Toyota)

11 ALIVE. (WPIX TV, Channel 11)

EVERYTHING YOU ALWAYS WANTED IN A BEER AND LESS. (Lite)

IT TASTES TOO GOOD TO BE TRUE. (Dr. Pepper)

WE DO IT ALL FOR YOU. (Mac Donald's)

ALL BANKS AREN'T THE SAME. (Manufacturers Hanover)

NOW THAT'S MORE LIKE IT! (Chevrolet)

WE HAVE SO MUCH TO GIVE! (Macy's)

THE SUPERSTAR IN RENT-A-CAR . (Hertz)

SEE SEAMAN'S FIRST.

TIME CAN BE BEAUTIFUL. (Longines)

BARNES AND NOBLE. OF COURSE. OF COURSE.

In addition to tracking the print and media sources which make contact every day, library PR people should keep up with the work of The Advertising Council. This organization is composed of representatives from major commercial agencies who volunteer their labors to approximately twelve campaigns of public concern a year. In recent years they have produced some of the most powerful television moments imaginable: the tearful Indian for "People start pollution. People can stop it"; the line for the United Negro College Fund, "A mind is a terrible thing to waste."

By writing to the Ad Council once a year, you may receive a copy of the bulletin listing their campaigns and the addresses of the campaign directors,* so that it is possible to obtain the printed materials which complement television spots. There is much creative material in these packets for "idea files." Not only are the pitch lines and graphics excellent, but the approaches to "selling" non-profit endeavors to the public are the finest models Madison Avenue can produce. Incidentally it may happen that the library will receive some excellent material for vertical files and exhibits as well.

Certainly librarians would not forget that they should read every advertising book that passes through the library as a new title, or as a gift (even if it is destined for discard). Any basic text will provide fundamentals which are better scanned once, than never considered at all. Articles in current magazines bring the generalized data of comprehensive texts to the specifics of recent campaigns.†

Anthologies of best commercials or prize winning graphics are well worth study. Each volume offers hundreds of easily adaptable ideas which cost someone else a pretty penny and have already demonstrated their power. Collections which organize on a "before and after" principle are particularly useful for they allow us to learn from others' mistakes, or benefit from the latest "improvements." Let's take one example:

Levy's Ovenkrust White Bread used to advertise on the assumption that caring mothers would welcome nutritional information. Ad copy was chock full of sound information. But supermarkets

---

* *Public Service Advertising Bulletin,* The Advertising Council, Inc., 825 Third Avenue, NY, NY 10022.

† For example: "New! Improved! Advertising," *New York Times Magazine* January 25, 1976, pp. 12 ff.; "Philip Morris: the hot hand," *Business Week,* December 6, 1976, pp. 60-3 ff.

17

and mothers alike were unimpressed. Why? Test Yourself. However spirited the verbiage, however interesting the facts do you *really* feel like reading this all?

> If you're buying white bread strictly by feel, you may be surprised by a few hard facts about "soft" breads. In the first place, it's a fact that the softest bread isn't necessarily the freshest. And it's also a fact that white bread without much body may be white bread without much nourishment. Bread that's a real food . . . packed solid with nutrition . . . is just bound to be fine, firm, and upstanding, with a texture that won't cave in under the butter knife. So why just feel around for good white bread? Dig deeper. Check the wrapper. Has the baker used unbleached flour? And wheat germ for nature's own goodness? And whole milk (instead of skim milk) for extra richness and nourishment? And pure golden honey (instead of sugar) to lift both the flavor and the energy quotient? If the wrapper says he has, you're getting your family really *good* white bread . . . and chances are it's Levy's Oven-Krust!

Probably not! When Doyle Dane Bernbach, Inc. turned the advertising technique away from this gentle over-verbosity to a catchy one liner — "You don't have to be Jewish to love Levy's — and away from skimpy drawings to intriguing photographs of ethnic faces, Levy's burst out of the New York deli world and into national supermarket success! Enjoy the brevity! The simplicity! And take heed next time a library blurb is due!

You don't have to be Jewish

to love Levy's
real Jewish Rye

Let us assume that you have an active, lively idea and word file at hand. What about a drawing? Once again, it is necessary to maintain an ongoing file of line drawings, so that artists — professional or otherwise — don't take a minute's time to draw a poorly conceived, poorly received representation of what *they* think a library is all about. It is far easier, cheaper and safer to control the design yourself by using prepared graphics.

Line drawing is simply a term used in the trade to mean pictures which contrast dark and light, without halftones. *Line drawing* includes shadings done with dots or lines of dark color. *Line drawing* does not include the gradations or halftones common to photographs. The definition is perhaps best clarified by several examples. All of the illustrations below are line drawings. A close squink shows that the shadowing areas are all composed of small dots and dashes of solid color.

Photographed below is a delightful cardboard lady. It contains many halftones. In order to print it, a separate screening process must be employed and the cost of production and the time required begin to rise.

If one simply takes the raw photograph without the screening process, the offset camera will translate the shadings as either black or white, and the following image results:

Photographs that have been previously printed in magazines or newspapers may be used, for they have already been screened. However, with each reprinting the quality decreases and the delicate shades become darker and darker.

For beginners then, it is best simply to avoid photographs of all kinds. Experienced hands frequently avoid them too, for in addition to costing additional money and time to produce, photographs are often much more difficult to use effectively.

Line drawings need not be printed in black ink on white paper. This *is* the best combination for subsequent clarity, but other dark colors will reproduce well: brown, red, dark blue. Avoid using drawings with extensive light shaded or light solid colors such as gray, pink, green, light blue or yellow. The rainbow given below should help you keep the offset camera color translation in mind. Note that the colors black, red, blue, green, brown and dark orange all become black. White, yellow, light blue become white and light green becomes a difficult melange.

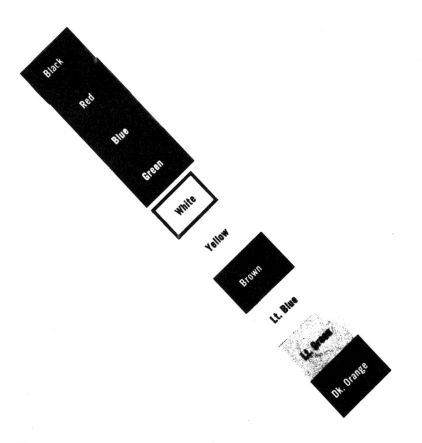

With the definitions of line drawing and the color possibilities clear, what precisely might be slipped into a picture file and where might these things be discovered? Librarians need go no further than the catalogues and gift books that deluge them every day. The person responsible for directing mail should be made aware of the desire for graphics and duplicate catalogues routed directly to the person in charge. If the supply of junk mail, gift and discard books, catalogues begins to dwindle, a picture file may be quickly replenished with one visit to the local recycling station.

Alert picture clippers look for the following things:

BORDERS: One handsome border, or portion thereof, can be all the design you need for a flyer.

CARTOUCHES: Small, ornamental frames into which one may put one's own words:

ISOLATIONS: Lettering or pictures from which you will use only a portion. The decorative lettering in the following heading is worthy of saving on the chance some portion might be used:

It's not impossible that one might want to use this as ERA, or Americans, or America, or I can.

Perhaps a picture, appealing in style and content, is buried within a larger picture. Save the entire thing on the assumption that the part can easily be isolated. For example, the sun in this Dover Coloring Book drawing:

OPTICAL ILLUSIONS: Always intriguing and popular, even the most common tricks still cause the observer to pause a moment and look twice:

For those who get the graphics bug and wish to spend a few dollars, there are also the following source possibilities for line drawings:

1. Dover Coloring Books. Those books in Dover's *Pictorial Archive Series* permit the use of up to four illustrations on any one project, free and without special permission. The diversity of available styles, quality of reproductions, and low cost (less than $2.00) make these volumes an outstanding value.

2. Copyright free picture books. There are a number of titles currently on the market. Unfortunately, they are frequently expensive, printed on both sides of the paper, and require extra time and money to use.

3. Transfer (presstype) symbols and border tapes. Among the many companies marketing these aids, Formatt seems to have the largest selection.

4. Clip art services. A word of caution before subscribing to any service. These are designed primarily for commercial agencies and frequently are utterly inappropriate for library use. If selection is not careful, the per-useable-picture cost can be extravagant.

Two last sources might be mentioned. If a person is so inclined, cutouts and doodles are quick, effective designs to use in printing. Librarians should save the glossy black covers that frequently come on catalogues, for it is excellent, fuzzless paper from which to snip a catchy motif. For example:

Likewise, doodles, given a dark border, can be very enticing:

But again, there are such quick sources for excellent, trouble free graphics, that it doesn't pay to snip or doodle if it doesn't come effortlessly.

4. READY? OFFSET PRINT IT!

In seeking the least expensive route to excellent quality print-ting, one inevitably comes to offset printing with "camera ready copy." Costs currently run $3.50-$4.00 per hundred, $12.50-$13.00 per thousand for basic black print on white bond, one side only.

"Camera ready copy" is material which is ready to print without further alteration or work. There are no substitutions or changes. Often the "copy" is in the form of a "paste up" sheet of paper on which headlines, text, drawings have been glued exactly as the customer desires them to be seen in the final product. This is the least expensive printing because the customer has assumed respon-sibility for the design and clarity of the product. Smudges, typos, er-rors of any kind in the copy become the buyer's fault, *not* the printer's. This burden is well worth shouldering in view of the cost saving, and it is not as awesome as it might sound.

Systems which have already acquired an electronic stencil maker and mimeograph equipment may use the same paste up prin-ciples as those for offset printing. Those systems which have relied on mimeograph alone, with typed and hand-done stencils, should seriously consider using a local offset establishment to do major pro-motional materials. Even with the advances of mimeograph in recent years, there is no way the finest machines can yet match the quality of offset printing. We are, after all, interested in improving our "nice guy," second best library image.

Let us proceed with the details of preparing a paste up sheet, for by now we are well supplied with ideas, words and pictures from our files. In order to condense the necessary information into workable form, the following dictionary of hints has been inserted. During the practical exercise that follows, and in the future, a student may quickly refer back to this section for guidance. Scan the definitions, but do not worry about specifics which don't make sense at the moment. Many points will become clear as you work later. The hints are designed to give beginners fine quality for the lowest cost, and therefore include some bias toward this end.

added costs	The following cost extra: cuts, folds, paper colors, ink colors, printing in more than one color, punched holes, staples, heavy/textured paper, printing on both sides. Some of these can be done by you or a volunteer. Some (expensive paper) should simply be avoided.
bibliography	An excellent, detailed booklet with paste up advice is available through local AM salesmen, or by writing Multigraphics Division, Addressograph Multigraph Corporation, 1800 West Central Road, Mt. Prospect, ILL 60056, and asking for *Preparing Copy for Camera.*
	For those who wish details on more advanced problems in printing, the following titles are highly recommended: *Printing It. A guide to Graphic Techniques for the Impecunious.* Clifford Burke. Berkeley, Wingbow Press, 1972. Available through Small Press Book Club, Box 100, Paradise, California 95969 for $3.00 plus 75¢ postage; *Pocket Pal. A Graphic Arts Book.* International Paper Company. Available through DOT Pasteup Supply Company, 1612 California St., Omaha, Nebraska 68102 for $2.00 plus 30¢ postage.
clarity	What you see is what you get. Take time to remove smudges, stray lines, flecks with opaque liquid. Rub off excess rubber cement. Avoid using xerox copy, colored paper and light ink drawings in your original paste up.

Dictionary

colors   Very dark colors will reproduce best: black,
                brown, red, dark blue. Avoid using light shaded or
                light solid areas such as gray, pink, green, blue,
                yellow.

enlargements   You may enlarge material with PMT (see below)
                for approximately $3.00 per 8½" x 11" sheet, less
                for smaller sizes.

folds   Folds cost money when done by the printer, and
                frequently waste a great amount of paper behind
                the scenes. Sometimes, there is no alternative;
                but if the job is one or two thousand (or less)
                discover the joys of doing it yourself. Clear off a
                large clean surface, get a number of staff, friends,
                volunteers or hanger-arounders into action! To
                achieve crisp, clean folds a folding bone (plastic
                ones are less than 50¢), kitchen spoon or round
                edged ball point pen casing will do wonders. The
                job speeds by, and if done in the public eye, is a
                great device for letting others know you can use
                volunteers every day for all kinds of tasks. Below
                are illustrated several of the most common folds:

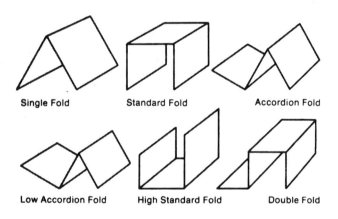

Single Fold   Standard Fold   Accordion Fold

Low Accordion Fold   High Standard Fold   Double Fold

format   Library literature frequently takes the following
                forms:

Handout (flyer, handbill) — a small sheet, unfolded, given out in the library and on the street as advertisement for events, services, programs.

Brochure (leaflet) — a folded handout with more complex or detailed information. Often used to summarize a library's services and requirements.

Poster — actually a handout of larger size and designed to be posted, rather than circulated person to person.

Invitations/announcements — somewhat more formal in content than handouts and frequently intended to be mailed in an envelope to specific individuals.

guidelines

Use a very light blue pencil, very gently! They do not need to be erased or opaqued as the offset camera will not see them.

instructions

Every job taken to a printer should have clear instructions (paper color, ink color, number, etc.) attached. One never knows when a part time worker, who is not familiar with your institution's likes and dislikes, will do the job. You have only yourself to blame if your verbal instructions are not followed.

layout and pasteup: *generalities*

A layout (the placement of print, type, open space) is "successful" if it attracts attention (usually done by the headline and graphic design) and if it achieves a clear understanding in a minimum of reading time. Certain principles will guide the beginner to an effective layout: simplicity, originality, legibility and balance.

Simplicity. Keep your facts to the essential minimum. It is not necessary to tell everything you know. A brief, clear statement of your message is far more enticing than a rambling essay. Being generous with open space and including a graphic of some kind will keep you from filling a sheet with words.

Originality. This need not be originality in the sense of creating something from nothing. It means using your stolen work, pictures, message with a unique twist. Organizing them with your own flair.

Legibility. Frequently people try to save time by printing headlines themselves, or by drawing little widgets and squiggles for pictures. Unless you know your excellence as a calligrapher and artist, don't do anything yourself. There are much quicker, easier routes.

Balance. Most people, if they remember to pause and consider the subject, have a natural intuition for this. Take your layout and look at it through one eye, or make a copy of your tentative layout on a copy machine. This, and your good sense will guide you toward a pleasant arrangement of open space, graphic and content message.

layout and pasteup: *specifics*

1. Decide on two-up, three-up, both sides, one side, number of folds.
2. Plan rough layout, leaving ½" margin.
3. Have materials reduced, enlarged.
4. Type copy with clean type on smooth white paper.
5. Presstype material for headlines.
6. Tape down layout sheet (one sheet for each side of printing) using t-square and triangle.
7. Mark guidelines with light blue pencil.
8. Glue material in place with rubber cement.
9. Touch up edges, smudges and marks with opaquing liquid (correction fluid).
10. Proof a final time. Make additions, deletions, substitutions by pasting new copy over existing material.

lettering

Use one of the *dry* pressure sensitive transfer lettering sheets. Choose a style which expresses the nature/philosophy of your organization or program. Do not rush out and buy a large quantity of type at one time, for it tends to dry out in a year (more or less, depending on how long it has been in the store), and becomes impossible to use. If you cannot find this type in an area office supply store, a list of major manufacturers may be found in the Appendix II. The companies will be glad to send a catalogue, inform you of the nearest dealer, and frequently will allow you to order supplies by phone or mail.

materials

To do efficient layout work you will need masking tape, light blue pencil, rubber cement, smooth white paper (never use corrasible bond), scissors, correction fluid, t-square and triangle. You do *not* need special light tables or paste up boards unless you move on to extremely detailed, high level work.

PMT

Photographic Mechanical Transfer will enable you to enlarge, reduce or reproduce copy without loss of quality. Price varies with the size, but 8½" x 11" is usually about $3.00. There is no way of doing this very specialized work yourself.

pencil

Don't use one.

pens

If you absolutely must use a ball point pen, use black, red or dark blue only. It would be better to keep a supply of black fine-line marker pens on hand for graphic work.

reductions

If you wish to reduce a picture, or section of copy, you may do this on a xerox 7000 machine for approximately 55¢ per sheet. Kodak's Ektaprint machine will do similar fine service. For better quality work, use PMT (see above). If, however, you wish to reduce an *entire* sheet, the printer can do this automatically, without extra charge.

typewritten copy

Always use a clean sheet of smooth white paper. Manual typewriters usually yield uneven and gray type, which reproduces with thin and broken letters. To avoid this, clean your keys and use a new black ribbon; or set the typewriter at stencil, and type through a sheet of carbon paper. Electric typewriters with carbon ribbons are best. If you do not own one, it is worth an hour's effort to call local schools, churches, businesses in search for a sympathetic being who will either type your copy as you dictate over the phone, or tell you when you might sneak in and use the electric typewriter. If you discover several possibilities, aim for the one which offers an IBM Executive, which has highly desireable proportional spacing.

You are now ready to make your pasteup for camera ready copy of a message to replace the Lewis Library brochure. The new version is intended to be both functional (listing important local telephone numbers) and informative (giving a zesty sampling of library programs and willingness to serve). It reuses the only admirable portion of the original brochure; namely, the architect's drawing. All the necessary print ingredients are provided on the following pages printed on one side only, so that you may actually snip and paste as the lesson proceeds. Come on! You *can* do it! The steps listed in the dictionary section for *layout and pasteup: specifics* (p. 32) will be followed and elaborated upon at each step.

BE A LIBRARY LOVER!

Last year we had Saturday Learning Experiments,
Eco-art for kids, Science Scenes for adults and
much, much more. We hope you'll drop in or
call to see what we're up to this year!

And remember! You can ask us ANY question,
even by phone! Big questions, little questions,
simple or complex. If there's an answer, we'll
find it for you!

WE REALLY WANT YOU TO BE A LIBRARY LOVER

Lewis Library 269 S. Central Avenue, Hopewell, NJ
609 - 466 - 0051

BE A LIBRARY LOVER!

Last year we had Saturday Learning Experiments,
Eco-art for kids, Science Scenes for adults and
much, much more. We hope you'll drop in or
call to see what we're up to this year!

And remember! You can ask us ANY question,
even by phone! Big questions, little questions,
simple or complex. If there's an answer, we'll
find it for you!

WE REALLY WANT YOU TO BE A LIBRARY LOVER

Lewis Library, 269 S. Central Avenue, Hopewell, NJ
609 - 466 - 0059

correction: 609 - 466 - 0051

EMERGENCY CALLS
      Ambulance and Fire..................... 466-1616
      If no answer, call 737-0101

POLICE DEPARTMENT 466-0892
      If no answer, call 737-2440

TAX COLLECTOR 466-0968
      Residence phone 466-1193
      Tuesday - 1 P.M. to 4 P.M.

WELFARE DIRECTOR
      Jeannette P. Hall 466-0214

LICENSE CLERK
      Elizabeth Hurley 466-0692
      18 Lafayette Street
      Dog, Hunting and Fishing, Marriage

COURTS
      Nicholas S. Castoro, Magistrate
      Dorothy Fish, Court Clerk 466-0724
      Sessions: Municipal Building
            Second and Fourth Tuesday,
            7:30 P.M.

GARBAGE COLLECTION
      Ray's Disposal 329-6273
          First District: Mon. and Thur.
          Second District: Tues. and Fri.
      Councilman Merritt McAlinden 466-0561

EMERGENCY CALLS
      Ambulance and Fire.................... 466-1616
      If no answer, call 737-0101

POLICE DEPARTMENT 466-0892
      If no answer, call 737-2440

TAX COLLECTOR 466-0968
      Residence phone 466-1193
      Tuesday - 1 P. M. to 4 P. M.

WELFARE DIRECTOR
      Jeannette P. Hall 466-0214

LICENSE CLERK
      Elizabeth Hurley 466-0692
      18 Lafayette Street
      Dog, Hunting and Fishing, Marriage

COURTS
      Nicholas S. Castoro, Magistrate
      Dorothy Fish, Court Clerk 466-0724
      Sessions: Municipal Building
                Second and Fourth Tuesday,
                7:30 P. M.

GARBAGE COLLECTION
      Ray's Disposal 329-6273
                First District: Mon. and Thur.
                Second District: Tues. and Fri.
      Councilman Merritt McAlinden 466-0561

PASTE UP EXERCISE

Step 1.   Decide on two up, three up, both sides, one fold, two folds.

It is possible to economize by printing handouts two or three to a page, in which case the pasteup sheet will have two or three items on one side (two up, three up). Pasteups for printing on both sides are done on two separate sheets, one for each side of printing. Pasteups for brochures with folds or cuts must allow ample space for columns, if folds and cuts are to coincide perfectly.

For this exercise, we will print two advertisements per page — two up — with printing on both sides.

Step 2.   Plan rough layout, leaving ½" margin around outer edge.

Most modern equipment will allow a little less than this, but while one is learning ½" is a safe rule.

Cut out headline, graphics and copy materials. Arrange them on a piece of 8½" x 11" paper. At this point we are simply getting an idea of where the basic parts will go. We have the following in mind: a telephone number card using half the sheet, with the architectural drawing of Lewis Library and the message on one side, the "pitch" line and telephone numbers on the reverse side. A hole will be punched in the center top.

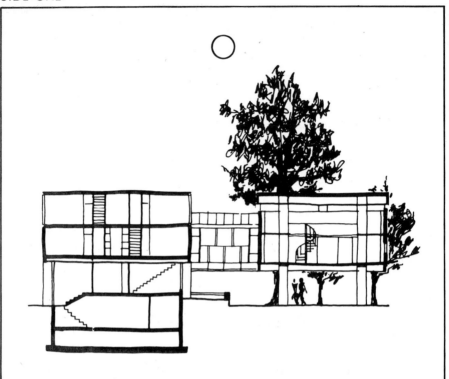

Last year we had Saturday Learning Experiments,
Eco-art for kids, Science Scenes for adults and
much, much more. We hope you'll drop in or
call to see what we're up to this year!

And remember! You can ask us ANY question,
even by phone! Big questions, little questions,
simple or complex. If there's an answer, we'll
find it for you!

WE REALLY WANT YOU TO BE A LIBRARY LOVER

Lewis Library 269 S. Central Avenue, Hopewell, NJ
609 - 466 - 0051

EMERGENCY CALLS
    Ambulance and Fire................... 466-1616
    If no answer, call 737-0101

POLICE DEPARTMENT 466-0892
    If no answer, call 737-2440

TAX COLLECTOR 466-0968
    Residence phone 466-1193
    Tuesday - 1 P. M. to 4 P. M.

WELFARE DIRECTOR
    Jeannette P. Hall 466-0214

LICENSE CLERK
    Elizabeth Hurley 466-0692
    18 Lafayette Street
    Dog, Hunting and Fishing, Marriage

COURTS
    Nicholas S. Castoro, Magistrate
    Dorothy Fish, Court Clerk 466-0724
    Sessions: Municipal Building
            Second and Fourth Tuesday,
            7:30 P. M.

GARBAGE COLLECTION
    Ray's Disposal 329-6273
          First District: Mon. and Thur.
          Second District: Tues. and Fri.
    Councilman Merritt McAlinden 466-0561

BE A LIBRARY LOVER!

In order to rough out this pasteup, use two sheets of paper (one for each side). Fold the sheets in half crosswise and open flat again — the folds being a reminder of the future cut, dividing each sheet into two equal sized handout cards.

On one sheet, place the architectural designs and the texts, two up, centered within the half sheet. You may wish to follow the example, or create a variation:

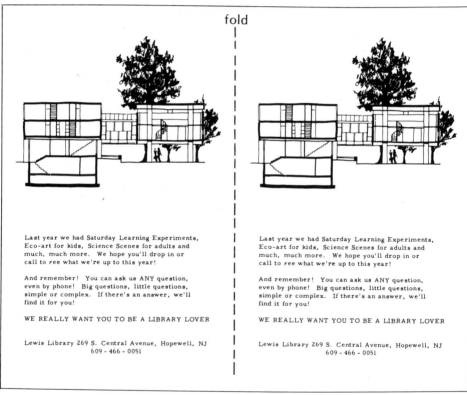

fold

Last year we had Saturday Learning Experiments, Eco-art for kids, Science Scenes for adults and much, much more. We hope you'll drop in or call to see what we're up to this year!

And remember! You can ask us ANY question, even by phone! Big questions, little questions, simple or complex. If there's an answer, we'll find it for you!

WE REALLY WANT YOU TO BE A LIBRARY LOVER

Lewis Library 269 S. Central Avenue, Hopewell, NJ
609 - 466 - 0051

Last year we had Saturday Learning Experiments, Eco-art for kids, Science Scenes for adults and much, much more. We hope you'll drop in or call to see what we're up to this year!

And remember! You can ask us ANY question, even by phone! Big questions, little questions, simple or complex. If there's an answer, we'll find it for you!

WE REALLY WANT YOU TO BE A LIBRARY LOVER

Lewis Library 269 S. Central Avenue, Hopewell, NJ
609 - 466 - 0051

11"

On the other sheet, place the telephone listings and the advertising lines.

46

fold

EMERGENCY CALLS
    Ambulance and Fire.................. 466-1616
    If no answer, call 737-0101
	EMERGENCY CALLS
	    Ambulance and Fire.................. 466-1616
	    If no answer, call 737-0101

POLICE DEPARTMENT 466-0892
    If no answer, call 737-2440
	POLICE DEPARTMENT 466-0892
	    If no answer, call 737-2440

TAX COLLECTOR 466-0968
    Residence phone 466-1193
    Tuesday - 1 P.M. to 4 P.M.
	TAX COLLECTOR 466-0968
	    Residence phone 466-1193
	    Tuesday - 1 P.M. to 4 P.M.

WELFARE DIRECTOR
    Jeannette P. Hall 466-0214
	WELFARE DIRECTOR
	    Jeannette P. Hall 466-0214

LICENSE CLERK
    Elizabeth Hurley 466-0692
    18 Lafayette Street
    Dog, Hunting and Fishing, Marriage
	LICENSE CLERK
	    Elizabeth Hurley 466-0692
	    18 Lafayette Street
	    Dog, Hunting and Fishing, Marriage

COURTS
    Nicholas S. Castoro, Magistrate
    Dorothy Fish, Court Clerk 466-0724
    Sessions: Municipal Building
        Second and Fourth Tuesday,
        7:30 P.M.
	COURTS
	    Nicholas S. Castoro, Magistrate
	    Dorothy Fish, Court Clerk 466-0724
	    Sessions: Municipal Building
	        Second and Fourth Tuesday,
	        7:30 P.M.

GARBAGE COLLECTION
    Ray's Disposal 329-6273
        First District: Mon. and Thur.
        Second District: Tues. and Fri.
    Councilman Merritt McAlinden 466-0561
	GARBAGE COLLECTION
	    Ray's Disposal 329-6273
	        First District: Mon. and Thur.
	        Second District: Tues. and Fri.
	    Councilman Merritt McAlinden 466-0561

BE A LIBRARY LOVER!   BE A LIBRARY LOVER!

8½ "

11"

Step 3.   Have materials reduced, enlarged, cropped.

At this point, if it is clear that something is simply an unworkable size, it could be enlarged or reduced. Original photographs could be cropped. Saving time and money, we will use the ingredients in the form which we find them.

Step 4.   Type copy

For the sake of this exercise, simply clip the text materials that are provided.

Step 5.   Presstype material for headlines.

Again, we can simply clip the line "Be a library lover!" for the lesson. When you are doing your own work, a few hints:

47

You may draw a light blue guideline on which to do your presstyping. Or you may presstype directly on a sheet of light blue lined paper to quickly achieve the necessary regularity. All the major catalogues have a page of instructions for using their type. In fact, however, a practice shot or two is worth more. This is fun! If it is not, if the letters are splitting or not sticking, try pressing lighter or heavier. If that does not solve the problems, you have probably been stuck with an old sheet of letters. Return it immediately and get a fresh replacement.

Step 6.   Tape down your layout sheets, using a t-square.

Place the crossbar of the t-square against the edge of a table, desk or carrel, and then align one of the paper edges with the long shaft of the t-square:

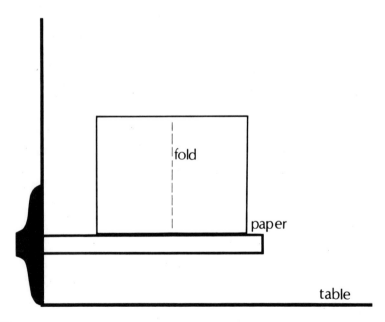

fold

paper

table

Using masking tape (scotch tape will make removal more difficult), tape all the corners securely.

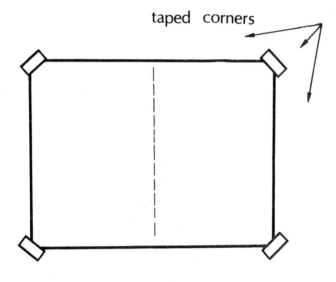

taped corners

Note: You may do this taping on a paste up board or light table, if you happen to have one. Otherwise, it is a luxury libraries can do without. Likewise, you may do this kind of work on prepared layout paper which has grid marks preprinted in light blue. These sheets are handy because they make alignment easy — by running a t-square or ruler across the sheet on the same number, one is assured of a straight line.

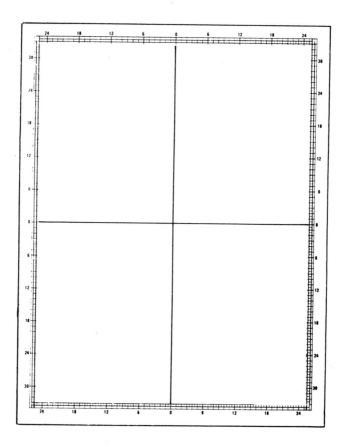

These sheets are very handy, but again, they are not necessary for routine work.

Step 7. Mark guidelines with light blue pencil.

Place the components in exact place, leaving equal margins on the left and right sides, and using the t-square to insure straightness of text materials. If one has a triangle, use the t-square along the bottom of text letters, and the triangle along vertical strokes (such as t's or simply along the outer edge of text:)

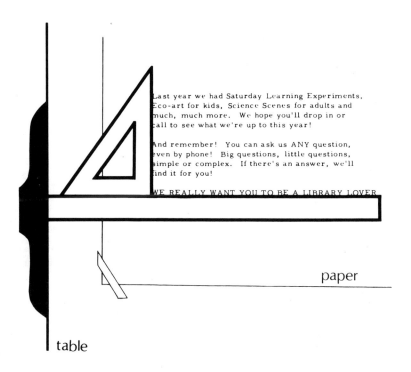

Inside the illustration:

Last year we had Saturday Learning Experiments, Eco-art for kids, Science Scenes for adults and much, much more. We hope you'll drop in or call to see what we're up to this year!

And remember! You can ask us ANY question, even by phone! Big questions, little questions, simple or complex. If there's an answer, we'll find it for you!

WE REALLY WANT YOU TO BE A LIBRARY LOVER

paper

table

Draw faint light blue guidelines around the corners of each piece of copy, once they are perfectly aligned. It is not necessary to line around the entire piece:

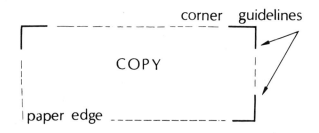

corner   guidelines

COPY

paper edge

It is also unnecessary to erase these lines, as light blue will not register with the offset camera.

Step 8.   Glue materials in place with rubber cement.

Do not use any other type of fixative. Rubber cement will not wrinkle the paper and will allow for easy removal in the event of an error.

Step 9.   Touch up layout sheet with opaquing liquid.

For important jobs, you may wish to do this with a magnifying glass. Ordinarily, the eye is good enough! Be sure to dot paper flecks, stray lines, finger print smudges, excess rubber cement which might have some dust trapped in it.

Step 10. Proof a final time.

It is tempting to skip this step, but *don't!* If there is an error, you need not redo the entire piece. Mistakes in presstype may be lifted off with the sticky side of scotch tape. Mistakes in copy may be retyped and glued directly over the area concerned. In this exercise, final proofing shows an error in the telephone number on one copy. Snip the correction and glue it *over* the existing mistake.

Finished? Congratulations! Now go "shopping" for an excellent printer.

Not all printers are the same! Some have better equipment. Some have more talent, consistency and concern. By shopping around, checking rates, looking at samples and talking with local people, you should be able to come up with the best. Remember, if a job is returned with fuzzy, blurry print, you should feel free to refuse the work. Either have it redone by the same printer, or take it this once and never return! If you have taken care with your pasteup, used electric typewriter copy and clear line drawings, the result should be crisp and clear print. Anything less is NOT acceptable!

5. CREATIVE PRINT DISTRIBUTION:
In house and in the real world

Let us assume that you now have a satisfactory brochure for general interest. What do you do with it? Very often the brochures end up in the back room, waiting for someone to ask for them or stacked invisibly in a library information center.

A more imaginative approach is needed if we are not to speak to the very same people over and over and over again. It is easy and obvious to mail a supply to realtors, welcome wagons and politicians. Social service agencies, PTA's religious organizations and local businesses should all receive copies *with personal notes,* even if it's a one line note. Bus depots, wash-a-mats, community centers, clinics and super markets are logical places for permanent distribution boxes or posters. Hopefully the brochure is versatile enough to be distributed at local fairs, festivals and parades.

It is necessary to be far more imaginative and personal than this for flyers advertising specific events. Say, for example, you are planning a series of Saturday Learning Experiments (SLEX). Topics include fruit bats, horse shoeing, folk dancing, European handball and the history of black fashion. You will want to distribute flyers both inside and outside the library.

For distribution within the library, we might take some hints from "point of purchase" advertising. POP, as it is called in the trade, is advertising on the spot of purchase — those cardboard stands, spinning watch cases, blinking beer lights, all strategically located and designed to make you buy on impulse. Our job is similar. People are not inclined to pick up papers from an inconspicuous pile unless they are told "this is exciting . . . this is for you!"

The Point of Purchase Advertising Institute once compiled the following list of various types of advertising displays:*

1. Deep-etched glass sign
2. Transparent plastic self-sticking sign
3. Decalcomania
4. Mobile
5. Plaque
6. Fabric banner
7. Illusion and projector units
8. Adhesive shelf tape
9. Molded ceramic figurine
10. Wall clock
11. Shelf topper
12. Enameled wall sign
13. Super basket units
14. Cash register displays
15. Heat rotor
16. Change trays
17. Rubber mats
18. Shadow box
19. Over-the-wire banner
20. Easel-back card
21. Tuck-in shelf card
22. Ad reprint holder
23. 3-D board units
24. Turntables
25. Departments
26. Demonstration stand
27. Merchandiser floor stand
28. Display carton
29. Jumble basket
30. Metal or wood racks
31. Card with motion
32. Mechanical book
33. Mechanical mannequin
34. Steady-light unit
35. Flashing-light unit
36. Moving letters
37. Diorama
38. Related item unit
39. Backbar menu sign
40. Indoor electric sign
41. Large itinerant units
42. Mirror units
43. Fluorescent units
44. Self-adhesive footprints
45. Changing scene units
46. Sound display
47. Blow-up product
48. Plastic reproduction of product
49. Molded plastic sign
50. Floor cutout
51. Window cutout
52. Checkout unit
53. Light-cord hanger
54. Self-adhesive strip for gondola molding
55. Window streamer
56. Self-selector units
57. Wallboards
58. Exhibition type units
59. Wall posters
60. Display shipping cartons

Our job, as with the television advertising, is to adapt these approaches for library use.

---

* *Principles of Advertising,* Edited by Woodrow Wirsig. Pitman Publishers, 1963, p. 324.

The SLEX program on bats could be appropriately advertised "in house" with low flying bat mobiles (#4). A few coat hangers (cut the curly parts off), some styrofoam packing cubes (painted black, if you have the time), some string and you're set.

Number 9 suggests the use of a molded ceramic figurine. Suppose, instead, you let the children's department have a special project some day and build a horse figure from the garbage they gather in the library neighborhood or parking lot. Politely, this is called building an eco-structure. In any case, you have created a program for kids, as well as an advertisement for your SLEX horse shoeing event.

Why not consider advertising the folk dancing with footprints everywhere (#44)? Up the bookshelves. On the ceiling. Across the checkout desk. On the windows. Try making barefoot prints of real feet and cutting them out!

Wall posters (#59) of famous sports figures are easy to obtain and could be hilarious with cartoon blips super-imposed, or presstyped directly on the poster. Perhaps O.J. Simpson saying: "Meet my friend Tom. He'll teach you SOME ball!"

"In house" advertising need not all be static display. Dressing the staff which is in public view is as much fun as it is effective. What better "come on" for your history of black fashions program than staff members donning dashikis for two weeks before the show?

Advertising specific events outside the library is often accomplished through posters, but flyers — when thoughtfully distributed — are an excellent means of bringing the details to those interested. For example, a supply of handball announcements should be given to local Y's, sports stores, athletic departments and athletic leagues. Personal distribution at local sports events (in handball uniform, of course!) would also be extremely useful. A flyer for Israeli folk dancing might be placed on the windshields of all cars at the local Jewish Community Center.

The point is, creating excellent verbiage is not enough. Care must be taken to get that message to fresh ears — those people who don't know us and don't like us, because they *know* we're just another library . . . cold . . . bureaucratic . . . impersonal.

6. PR BEGINS AT THE DOOR: Exhibits and Posters

At most libraries, visitors are confronted immediately with stiff formality. It is not unusual to be met with two or three negatives before even opening the door: No Smoking. No Eating. No Pets. The circulation/charge out desk is almost always placed by the main entrance. Occasionally there are some locked glass exhibit cases somewhere within eyeshot. Then too, there is row after row of straight, rigid shelving.

Library workers forget how intimidating all of this is. They tend to think of it kindly because they have a happy job, and know that the library is more than desks and shelves and locks. But the newcomer doesn't know any more than he sees. A quick polaroid shot from the doorway of a library will reveal in static, unadulterated form just exactly what the visitor sees. Inviting? Warm? Human? Often the picture confirms the lifeless bureaucracy (check out desk and big brother making sure the rules are obeyed) and formality (you may look, but please don't you touch) of the negative national stereotype. Many folks have turned heel and run from just such a vista as this:

Sinclair Gauldie, in his book *Architecture,* interprets the general power of a structure as follows:

> In the shadow of a very large building the sensitive observer is rather like a small boy in the presence of his headmaster. The thing looms over him, it claims authority by its very size, and he enjoys not only a sensation of relief but a heart-warming experience when it indicates, if only by a friendly nod, that he is something more than a beetle at its feet.*

It is exactly this warm friendly nod that is needed in libraries. If we get the ear of a non-user and convince him to come to the library, we don't want him to flee without a fair sample of our service to him. We must engage him at the door, and allow him to share and participate in our unknown realm until he feels it is his own.

Most library institutions will not, or cannot move the circulation monitor away from the front door. But they certainly could dramatically mollify negative impressions by adding touchable, lovable exhibits and friendly, personal posters.

EXHIBITS: materials and ideas

In a recent article on creativity, the following question was given: "Write down all the uses you can think of for a junked automobile"† A list of 6-14 was average. Fifteen or above supposedly indicates superior originality. This approach is not unreasonable when developing concepts for exhibits. If we force ourselves to think for a moment, there is at least one exhibit for every item we see around us. Test yourself right now. Look around. Isn't there a chair, a ladder, a rug, a basket . . . something you can think of a "pitch line" for to use at the front of your library. From my vantage point at the moment I see the following: cranberries, stones, tin cans in the trash basket and the family tent.

It is easy to conceive of the following freewheeling, touchable exhibits by which to break up the rigidness of the front desk scene: 1) A table full of stones, glue, paint, paint brushes and several examples of stone sculptures. With simplified instructions, patrons can easily "do it" themselves. 2) A table full of crumpled tin cans, paint and paint brushes with several tin can people and perhaps the line: Bent out of shape? Relax with us! 3) The tent pitched in full glory with an invitation to "Come on in!" 4) Edibles made from cranberries (staff

---

* Gauldie, Sinclair. *Architecture,* NY, Oxford, 1969, p. 32.
† *Science News,* April 23, 1977, vol. III, no. 17, p. 268.

willing, of course) distributed free at some hour of the day: free recipes and the history of cranberries distributed at other times.*

This sort of exhibit, which invites and surprises and involves the observer, is easy to convert into a program. One day, for example, an artist could do his thing with stone sculptures at the display table. This creates a knot of people, which tends to gather more and more people. The awkwardness and uneasiness of the newcomer is quickly dispelled.

But suppose the supply of domestic exhibitables is exhausted. The entire staff is drained. There is a never ending supply available for a bit of begging and "stealing." If you see something that is worthy of exhibiting, ask for it! You may ask in person, by letter or by phone. There are virtues in each approach. Your wildest dreams are quite likely to come true with an enthusiastic, creative letter to big time manufactureres and institutions. If it's a local person or institution, try begging in person. It's very hard to say no to a librarian. Capitalize on the world thinking that librarians are gentle and helpless!

Canvas the community's disposal containers (they are frequently hidden from full view — try harder!) and by all means take materials you need from them! Carpeting, fabric, toys, wood, styrofoam, tubes, cardboard, tires, 2 x 4's, you name it . . . is all available FREEEEE for imaginative exhibits.†

Let us assume that the concept and materials are in order for an exhibit. Certain principles — beyond the desire to render the library more inviting — will insure a lively exhibit.

1. Never use an item which you will regret having stolen, broken or injured in some way. Open exhibits are very rarely harmed. But discretion is better than regret.

2. Each exhibit must have one, and only one concept. Do not try to say everything at once. There will be other exhibits and other times by which to refine the messages. Communicate succinctly.

---

* Ocean Spray Cranberries, Inc. has excellect material available free. A great many other producers do too. It takes only a letter of inquiry to discover.

† For an excellent article on scrounging for exhibit materials see the *Mother Earth News* reprint in Appendix III.

3. Usually a clear poster is in order, to very simply state the pitch. Again: Brevity is not only a virtue, it is absolutely essential. Details on postermaking methods follow in this chapter.

4. One exhibit item will do many things. The tent might be used for surprise value alone. It could also be the scene of the week's story hours, or the distributing point for free brochures on the state's camping grounds, or the advertisement for a slide program on Camping through the Himalayas, or the stage for an ecology puppet show, or the home of Halloween Witch Hermina. Anything goes!

5. The bigger the better. In the world of clutter and confusion, one sure way of getting attention without paying, is to take up a lot of space. Things like rubber boats, pieces of furniture, indoor gardens, mannequins, papier mache monsters, bicycles, wheelbarrows, cars, motors — are the idea.

6. The livelier the better. Virtually any animal should be welcome at the library exhibit center! Hatch a few, if you can't find someone's to borrow.

7. Aim at every age. We are all kids at heart! And therefore, it is not at all difficult to produce something with genuine appeal for everyone!

8. Give away as much free information as possible. If you have a broken cane chair, write for leaflets on how to recane furniture. If you are baking bread, or simply offering bread samples, distribute a quality bread baking book.

This is a good place to note that librarians should always grab interesting pamphlets that they see in motels, restaurants, stores, airports. Then, when the mood is right, fire off letters begging for multiple copies of the good ones (even if they are meant to be sold). As these come in, the exhibits can flow along smoothly.

9. There is a sort of snowball and pendulum rhythm to exhibiting. Once the principle of open, free exhibits is established, many offers will present themselves without any effort on the library's part. The enthusiasm for plants or animals or musical instruments will snowball at an astounding pace. Then, at some moment, the pendulum will start swinging back in another direction, with a new concept. The momentum will start up again and push into a new sphere of knowledge.

10. Don't spend time or money. The point of inviting exhibits is to break up the dull monotony of library entrances. Change and excitement are vital. A great expenditure of money is ridiculous and unnecessary. A great expenditure of time may be tempting (exhibits are more fun than overdues), but is equally as ridiculous and unnecessary. The most difficult part is getting an idea and making one poster to express it clearly. The rest is a question of transportation.

It may seem "unprofessional" to be carting around chicken feed or gathering tin cans, simply to provide a warm greeting for some unknown library patron. But professionalism, as one company has stated it, is more than education, more than experience, more than training. It is a state of mind.* Librarians must care. We must care that all are welcome . . . that all can understand how the institution serves the tiny individual . . . that the national stereotype be proven wrong. Exhibits are a small price to pay in terms of our most genuine concerns. Yes! Yes! The library cares!

POSTERS: Intro

Simplicity, originality, legibility and balance are as vital to success in postermaking, as they are to effective printing. Once again, it is essential to say everything as simply and briefly as possible. Once again, the lettering should probably not be done by hand using instead presstype, vinyl peel letters or poster maker machine printing.†

Posters give an individual library a chance to show its true colors. They can be done with a uniqueness and flair that is not attainable in mass marketed products. They can say exactly what the library wishes to say, rather than what someone else thinks the library should be saying. They can swiftly smash the interpersonal silence barrier and aid significantly in humanizing a visually negative situation. It is "easier" to pay a dollar and order a pre-fab message. But there is a lengthy time delay before that poster appears in the library and the message might even be false or misleading! Consider such recent favorites: "Free people. Free Libraries", and "Get Ahead. Read." Are libraries free? Does reading an Avalon romance help to get a body ahead?

---

* Walter S. Robbins Associates, Inc. 201 East 5oth St., NY, NY.
† Presstype has been discussed on p. 32. Economical vinyl peel letters are available from Presto for $1.29 per sheet. Poster making machines are somewhat expensive; but their versatility and excellence make them, in the long run, an extremely wise investment.

POSTERS: One of a kind

Libraries frequently have need for "one of a kind" posters. It may be for formal informational/directional signals, or informal program announcements, or friendly notes.

Directional posters should always be done neatly, in large type, with a consistent bright color theme so that patrons can easily scan all the orange signs hanging from the ceiling, for example, in order to find what they need. Attractive borders may be added with a yardstick and magic marker, without detracting from the central information.

Warm personal words should appear in libraries from the front door to the magazines, microfiche cabinets to fiction shelves, information desk to special collections. A quick canvas of library staff members will reveal what most patrons request help with, and where they ask for it. Place encouraging signs at those points (on desks, walls, shelves, people, ceilings, clocks, copy machines). For every person who asked, many more were too embarrassed or afraid. Speak naturally. Library jargonese is for the back room. A few possibilities:

Think I won't help? Try me!
Ask! I'm here to help.
If you think nobody cares . . . try us!
We care. We share. Ask.
Need help? That's our job.
We've got your answer!
How can we help, if you don't ask?
We're not too busy for YOU!
What's the problem? We'll help.
Catalog got you down? Let's tackle it together.
Come on. Ask.
Questions are our business.

The fundamental techniques for lively, one-of-a-kind, informal posters may be developed quickly by making a few mini picture posters. All that is necessary is a good supply of interesting magazine pictures, some construction paper (maybe) and presstype (or vinyl peel letters). Leaf through the pictures and allow them to inspire a line. This is far easier and usually more whimsical than imposing a preconceived line upon a picture. Let us take a few possibilities for a poster to replace the barrage of negatives at the library's front door. We are trying to be inviting, to crash the institutional barrier, to say "Come on in!"

PICTURE	PITCH LINE
Boxer delivering k.o. blow	Don't knock us til you try us!
Two kids, rear view, arm in arm	Please! Think of us as a friend.
Psychedelic head design	We're different. Give us a try.

Rubber cement will glue the trimmed picture in place on construction paper without shrinkage. Presstyping may be done directly on the picture, or on the backing. The entire procedure (given an active picture file) has probably taken less time than the reading of catalogs, processing of vouchers, writing of checks and other professional rigamarole involved in ordering a poster. Change, quintessential ingredient for maintaining interest, is easy and inexpensive to achieve.

Informal messages have added excitement if they are presented on unlikely surfaces. With presstype or vinyl lettering, it is possible to speak on kites, mirrors, maps, doors, desks, records, mylar, fans, tin cans, newspaper, oil barrels, paintings, magazine covers, fabric, wastecans, oversized posters, calendars, clocks, chairs, shelves, blow up photos, saw horses, carrels, automobiles . . . For example:

Mirror:	Created to serve . . . you!
Oil Barrel:	Library power. Still cheap.
Kites:	We fly for you.
Maps:	Lost? We'll find a way.

Don't throw out *anything* until you have decided that it is not useful for exhibits or poster backing. Save those junk mail poster sized ads. Grab that roll of newsprint or computer printout paper. Horde those lifesized cardboard people and animals. Ask for that corrugated cardboard in the drug store window. With a ready supply of postermaking materials, any notion, any announcement, can be imaginatively converted to print in just a few minutes.

POSTERS: Multiples

Multiple posters advertising the library or library events are more difficult than the flamboyant one-of-a-kind. Such posters usually carry more detailed information and are in direct competition with other posters and messages. The following magic marker special affords an excellent lesson in what not to do!

GRAND OPENING

Don't forget to visit the new branch library located 400 yards west of the "CENTER". Yes What an opening! We will start June 18 with all day

STORY HOURS

BY

Library Staff

food & snacks

come as you ..."

BOOK SALE
BENEFIT "FRIENDS"
10¢   25¢   50¢ $1.00

DON'T MISS IT!

MOVIES IN THE COURTYARD!

Using the criteria of simplicity, originality, legibility and balance (see *layout,* p. 31-2) this poster fails dramatically. The clutter of so many poorly printed words at varying angles, interspersed with midget drawings, presents the busy passerby with too much to absorb at a glance. The central message — the celebration of a new library — is obscure. The factual details — exact time, address — are nowhere to be found. It is simply too much to ask of anyone to stop, ferret out the given information, and then fill in the blanks for the missing details.

It might be noted, that the very content of this poster is not as original as it could be. Certainly if ever there is a chance to count upon guaranteed press coverage for the library, it is at the opening of a new branch. This library has offered a fairly mild, typical sounding schedule of events. The spark and excitement of "birthing" is indistinguishable from the haunting national stereotype. Libraries are "supposed" to have story hours. They are "supposed" to have films. Those who doubt this last statement will enjoy the following line from a newstory on an outstanding library Energy Day: "Of course there will be the obligatory film, this one from HUD about solar heat."* And finally, libraries very commonly have book sales.

The administrators and board of this library should have taken a moment to select a theme, cluster several fascinating activities around the idea, develop a symbol or logo for the entire happening, and done a first rate job for this once in a lifetime affair. Suppose the concept were: We're taking off! Come along! With a little arm twisting, a large number of events might be organized without cost to the library:

TAKE OFF BY FOOT:	Walking tour of historic Hopewell with President of Historic Society.
BY BIKE:	Ten mile ride to Washington's Crossing Park. Bring a brown bag picnic.
BY FIRE ENGINE:	Round trips to firehouse. Snacks courtesy of Auxiliary.

* *Trenton Times,* May 27, 1977, p. C1.

BY HORSE & BUGGY:	Round trips to Mombaccus Dairy. Guided tours of bottling plant.
BY ANTIQUE CAR:	Parade and exhibition.
BY HELIUM BALLOON:	Balloons to be released with names and addresses on return postcards for finders to mail back. Prize for the one who got farthest away!
BY CANOE:	12 mile trip on Raritan Canal.
BY ROCKET:	Models to be fired from library lawn.
BY UNICYCLE:	Demonstrations and lessons.
BY KITE:	All day kite flying in library field. Judging at 3 p.m. for numerous categories.

An arrow would be easy to execute as a motif for all the publicity work. It might be snipped out of dark paper:

Or, printed quickly on a poster maker:

Or, "borrowed" from a clip art service:

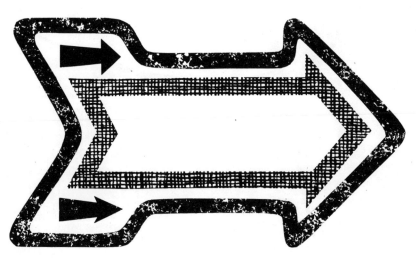

Or, presstyped:

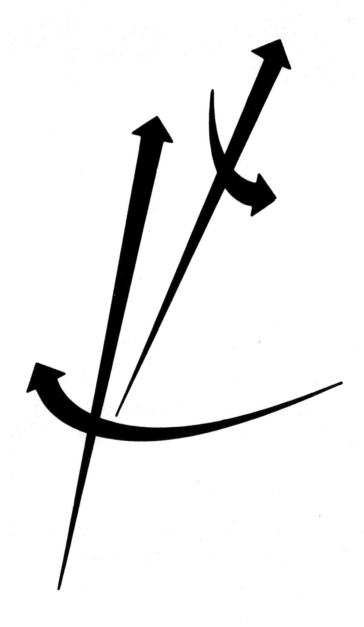

Or, taken from a non-copyrighted picture book:

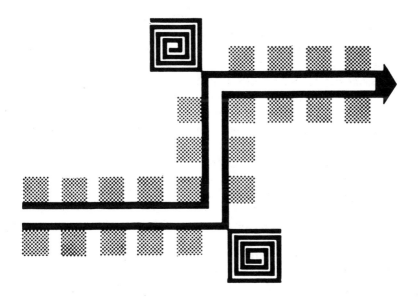

Or, doodled:

Complete details for the specific events might be printed on small sheets and distributed from pockets on the posters.

Offset posters are as easy and inexpensive to produce in quantity as the handouts discussed in the previous chapter. The pasteup process is the same. Posters can be printed on legal size or even larger paper. Handouts could be mounted on colorful posterboard and save the time spent on a separate design. In either case, offset printing can be quickly dolled up with volunteer labor pasting cut outs or daubing a splash of paint. These touches should not be fussy and time consuming. They should be broad, sweeping strokes designed to attract attention.

Postermaking machines are invaluable to printing large numbers of posters "in house." Again, hand done touches are useful. Experiment with cleaning the roller on clean sheets of posterpaper. Then the next time around, posters can be made using these swirly roller designs as background. Time and energy willing, these posters may even be cut out in interesting shapes.

Children's art may easily be generated in story hours and used as background for either offset or postermaker posters. The appeal of children's art is universal. The warmth, humor, color and insight of a child's mind engages the crustiest of cynics and forces a smile.

Just as every library should keep a ready mailing list of newspapers and social organizations, so too should they maintain an active list of bulletin boards or announcement centers in the community. Churches, schools, supermarkets, bus stations, airports, factories, medical centers, social agencies, shopping centers, ball parks, are but a few places to check out. Once the list is in hand, volunteers can easily get the library's message to a far ranging, diverse audience. There are many unknown faces out there who would just love to "Come along," on a library take off, if only they had known.

7. PUBLIC SPEAKING:
How not to live up to expectations

Librarians get frequent invitations to do book talks, class visits and guided tours of the library. Often it is as hard to be enthusiastic about doing one of these things, as it is for others to sit through. Quality book talks take genuine pedagogical talent and more hours to prepare than most librarians have to give. Classes usually know the potential usefulness of reference books and card catalogues. The chance to point out the children's collection, the magazines, the New Jerseyana collection, the microfiche drawers one more time, is not usually a happy prospect.

But it is necessary to rethink these grungy speaking opportunities and develop fresh approaches, for they represent the most important public relations channel libraries have. Any time a "librarian" stands before a group, he has the most time and the most flexibility in presenting the library's philosophy. He also has the potential for *two way* communication — a chance not only to speak clearly and passionately himself, but a chance to listen to user and non user as well. It is NOT necessary to live up to dismal expectations. It is not necessary to actually deliver a mediocre book talk or lecture monotonously for an hour on the card catalogue. Let's not simply fill time. Let's *use* it!

Consider the task of explaining the library to a group of high school kids. All too often we try to sell them on looking things up in the card catalogue. But the catalogue is a riddle, a game — an object which requires great humor, patience and forgiveness. Afterall, who would guess that salt free diets are not to be found under diet? Or that tai chi is listed under physical fitness? Or the autobiography of Malcolm X is only under X? Better to put the visitors in a relaxed frame of mind with an educational game or two, showing them that librarians think this is all funny and frustrating too!

The SAME GAME is a pleasant introduction to the principle of subject headings. It forces participants, in a most delightful way, to search for the common denominator of a collection of goodies. This is, in short, what one does when one checks for books by their subject. Take a number of items (3-10) which have a common trait — all have white on them, all are wood products, all have points, all have a round edge, all begin with the letter "j", and put each set of "sames" in a separate bag. For example, one bag might contain a pennant, a wine bottle, a train schedule, a license plate and a campaign election button. Another bag might have a bird house, a cork, the *Guinness Book of World Records,* and some turpentine.* Dump the bags out, one at a time, with the challenge to find the similarity. Enthusiasm for the sport is quick to burgeon.

Then, capitalizing on this joyous spirit, switch to the BIG BOOK GAME. Take interesting reference books and place one question which can be answered by a given book on a paper inside that book. Using the concepts developed above — that is, thinking of the category or subject heading which will cover the subject of the question — let each person try to find the answers, passing books around as quickly as the solutions are found. Naturally, when preparing these questions, try to be as tricky as possible, discovering curious, unpredictable headings or facts. It doesn't hurt to have a ridiculous "award" ready for the hero that finds most of the answers — you might even steal the *Guinness Book* from the previous game.!

These games are entertaining. They are also exceedingly instructional. And the supreme principle of try, try, trying again is pleasantly reinforced. The ultimate message — PLEASE, when you run out of tricks, ask your favorite librarian — is easily delivered and easily *believed* once this ground work is completed.

Perhaps there is a group of senior citizens or foreigners visiting the library. What is expected is a routine book talk and a walking tour of the library. Nobody really wants a book talk. They are requested because a busy program chairman gets out of doing a program himself and he *knows* librarians do these things. A different program would be welcomed! One logical possibility is to have these groups join in a story hour using materials already prepared. For example:

---

* You guessed it! The first group all has print; the second are all wood or wood products!

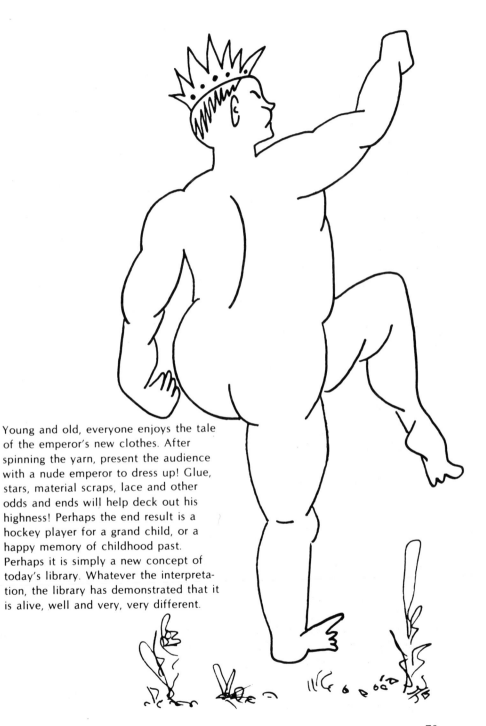

Young and old, everyone enjoys the tale of the emperor's new clothes. After spinning the yarn, present the audience with a nude emperor to dress up! Glue, stars, material scraps, lace and other odds and ends will help deck out his highness! Perhaps the end result is a hockey player for a grand child, or a happy memory of childhood past. Perhaps it is simply a new concept of today's library. Whatever the interpretation, the library has demonstrated that it is alive, well and very, very different.

There are occasions when librarians must become podium pounding public speakers — PTA requests at National Book Week time, civic organizations requesting a review of library services, boards desiring an official budget presentation. Some people are born with the eloquence and grace to handle these opportunities. Most need every crutch available in order to produce memorable, stimulating speeches.

The easiest solution to this problem is to prepare an excellent general slide tape to supplement public addresses on specific topics. This process is not as difficult or technical as it first might seem. Take out the file of advertising lines that you have prepared and maintained. Refresh your memory by running through all the possibilities and perhaps exchanging ideas with another library worker. Jot down a rough story skeleton, using both the advertising lines and your own "connectors." Remember that you do not have to use everything that you like! Complexity is not a virtue! There must be a message — a message that is clear and honest — articulated with the greatest brevity and humor possible.

A mini-story-line for a slide tape might read something like this:

Libraries used to be like this.
Some of them still are.
But not Lewis Library.
We're different.
Very different.
We really want to help.
Whoever you are.
Whatever you need.
Sharing is our business.
Lewis Library . . .
Created to serve . . .
You!

There are 40 words in this sequence. 13 of them (30%) came directly from the ad worksheet inspirations earlier in this book. With a rich file of verbiage, it doesn't take long to put a reasonable message together.

Now it is necessary to assemble pictures or mini posters to parallel the story. A Kodak Ektagraphic visual maker is invaluable for converting flat pictures, print or posters into slides.* With an active

---

* For details on the Visual maker and its use, see Appendix IV.

picture file and a day of picture taking at *library programs* (remember: most static library pictures are not particularly inviting), there will be more than enough material for use.

Let us run through the lines again and suggest a few picture possibilities:

Libraries used to be like this:	Your own library in the past Monastery libraries Medieval chain libraries
Some of them still are:	Any dismal library Locked book cases Quiet signs Negative signs Any grey abandoned book and desk Prison bars
But not Lewis Library	Any big glamorous building Your own library Exciting op art Fireworks Parade
We're different	Busy library pictures Zany visual maker pictures Librarians in costume Animals People pyramid of staff Optical illusion
Very different	Librarians climbing book shelves Exceptionally inviting library signs Unusual programs Any crowd List of outstanding library events Visual maker shots of gorgeous models Librarian reading comic book Superman, Wonderwoman

We really want to help	Reference desk with "Please bother me" sign
	Librarians on floor or on stilts looking for books
	Librarians putting on coats, carrying 50 books, buckling boots
Whoever you are	Collage of animal/people faces
	Computer picture
	Baby picture
	Workers in uniforms of various types
Whatever you need	Library scenes
	Pictures of food, swimming pools, cars, puddles, musical instruments, sports equipment, term papers, moon, space, starvation
Sharing is our business	Circulation desk with staff on top
	Hands cutting cake, pie, apple
	Two people in a potato sack
	Two people handcuffed
	Many people working around one table
	Person pushing wheelbarrow of books
Lewis Library . . . created to serve you!	Numerous faces of every race, age, style possible

Once the pictures and lines are assembled, select a reader to deliver the lines. Dress rehearse the lines, together with the visuals and a small "audience" — preferably a non library audience. Evaluate the project candidly: 1) Does the presentation catch the eye? 2) Does it catch the ear? 3) Is there a clear, honest, interesting statement made about a specific library? 4) Have you made a significant contribution toward exploding the national stereotype?

If the program passes these tests, then go ahead, number the slides, and commit the message to tape (either a simple voice tape, or a voice and music combination, if possible). A small note, click or chime might be included for each change of slide, so that no "thinking" is necessary in order to run the show.

Sometimes it is convenient and/or necessary to provide some sort of "microphone" through which the public can speak back to libraries. Asking at the end of a speech, "Does anyone have any questions?" frequently yields an embarrassing silence. Even putting the audience at ease with a line like, "Last time somebody asked me if . . ." may not always be enough. If this problem is attacked in the very beginning of a program with a form: "Give us your dreams. What could your library do for you?" there is a guaranteed response, which can be discussed with warmth and excitement. Formal as this procedure may sound, it *does* reveal how eager and responsive you are for any kind of suggestion. And if the suggestions are thoughtfully, publicly considered, it is an outstanding demonstration that the library really does care.

8. AND SO TO DREAM . . .

A few tricks mastered and any librarian is on the way to impecunious PR success. There are but three minimum requirements:

1. *Keep picture files.* Line drawings for offset work and
color photography for mini
posters and visual maker slides
2. *Collect things.* For poster backgrounds and for exhibiting
materials
3. *Keep advertising idea files.* For pitch lines to use in
brochures, posters, slide tapes

All that remains is to be staunchly devoted to the virtues of clarity, brevity and honesty.

The dream that is "sold" must come from within. No book, no lesson, no manual can prescribe the exact ingredients, passion and words for another institution's PR message. Interpretations of "library" may be as varied and splendid as the librarians who serve and care. Each library will have its own dream, its own distinctive message. We offer, in closing, a few thoughts on the heritage that *is* common to all libraries, that *should* be part of the national stereotype . . . a foundation upon which to build dreams . . .

LIBER

Trace for a moment the Latin word *liber* and discover not only the word *book,* but also the word *bark;* more precisely, *inner bark.*

There are three layers of bark to every tree: the epidermis, or outer bark, composed of dead tissues which protect the inner living parts; the middle bark, or cortex, containing chlorophyl and continually being replaced by the outer bark; and the inner bark, where delicate sieve tubes carry food throughout the system. It is the growing of the inner bark which causes the outer bark to stretch and tear, graciously departing, leaving behind a larger, stronger tree.

Librarians are that thin layer of life between wood and bark, between book and institution. Librarians are responsible for continued growth and vibrance. Librarians must pressure outer protective covers (and people) to yield to the new and the living.

Celebrate the original Latin heritage of the profession with a fresh institutional concept: inner barkians will grow; outer barkians will yield. Without the natural balance, the tree is dead. It is a fact: If it doesn't move, it isn't alive!

Libraries are for living . . .

Appendix I. REMINDERS

Note: The checklist below reflects some of the very fine, commonsense advice given in *Pointers for Publicists. How can NAB's story Emerge from a Mountain of News?* This non-copyrighted pamphlet was published for "in house" use by the metro offices of the National Alliance of Businessmen and touches on many of the obvious but oft ignored basics of public relations work.

1. The competition for Press recognition and coverage is intense. The decisions about what "is" and "is not" news are made by individuals. Find the most direct line of personal communication with these people. They are, after all, quite human and have a tough job.

2. Have something worth saying. Say it CLEARLY and SIMPLY.

3. Use specific events as a vehicle for comments on the library's general goals and dreams. Create an awareness of what the institution is trying to do.

4. Clarity is easily achieved if the old journalistic questions: Who? What? Why? When? Where? How? are answered.

5. The first paragraph of any notice is the most important. Your "handout" will be a "throwout" when a busy person reads the first paragraph and learns nothing.

6. Personal meetings with editors and reporters deserve TOP PRIORITY. State clearly what the library is trying to do, why you are trying to do it and how you are going about it.

7. Give special attention to the people in charge of free public service ads in area print, radio and television. You could be in for a bonanza.

8. Don't wait for big news to compile a press list of every possible carrier of news. Be sure to track down the myriad of local newsletters and newspapers printed by PTA's, churches, ethnic groups, senior citizens, the Chamber of Commerce, Recreation Council and schools (public and private).

9. Remember the KISS rule when speaking in public. Keep It Simple, Simon! Use short words, short speeches and a friendly, conversational tone.

APPENDIX II. Presstype and Pasteup Supply Sources

Note: If the Yellow Pages and a few calls are not sufficient to identify a local source for your supplies, write to any of the manufacturers listed below and request their catalog and dealer list. If there simply is no outlet close by, consider doing your business by mail with Pressure Graphics or Dot Pasteup Supply Company.

Even if you know where to buy your materials, you might want to write one or two of these companies anyway. You'll find yourself on some neat graphics mailing lists!

C-Thru Graphics
6 Britton Drive
Bloomfield, Connecticut 91605

Chartpak
1 River Road
Leeds, Massachusetts 01053

DOT Pasteup Supply Company
1612 California Street
Omaha, Nebraska 68102

Formatt
Graphic Products Corporation
3601 Edison Place
Rolling Meadows, Illinois 60008

Letraset USA Inc.
33 New Bridge Road
Bergenfield, NJ 07621

Pressure Graphics, Inc.
1725 Armitage Court
Addison, Illinois 60101

Zipatone, Inc.
150 Fencl Lane
Hillside, Illinois 60162

APPENDIX III. Think scrounge for Materials
A Mother Earth News Reprint
Courtesy The Register and Tribune Syndicate, Inc.
Des Moines, Iowa

How many times have you been frustrated by a craft magazine article which called for "scraps you have around your shop?" It's tough enough to buy building materials for your main projects, let alone have all the scraps you need for those one-evening projects.

Well, you can become wealthy with 2 x 4s, odd sheets of plywood, lengths of molding and other lumber and hardware if you learn to scrounge.

No, that doesn't mean "steal." Scrounging is recycling — using materials that others don't want and are glad to get rid of.

Not only can it be financially advantageous to you, it's sound ecological practice for the planet. This country throws away, burns or otherwise destroys hundreds of millions of board feet of usable lumber every year. Scrounging simultaneously lessens our disposal problems and cuts demand for new materials.

GOOD SOURCES of materials are all around you, most often in buildings awaiting demolition. Wrecking contractors seldom have time to do anything other than level the homes, offices, apartments or whatever and cart all the material away as quickly as possible.

That's wasteful. Just keep your eyes peeled for signs of urban renewal, redevelopment or house wrecking. Locate the supervisor on the job and ask his permission to haul old materials away. He might charge you a fee, but more often than not, he'll tell you to go right ahead — for nothing.

Kent McKeithan of Pittsburgh did just that. He paid $3 for unlimited rights to salvage anything he chose from a two-story frame house. He went in with a claw hammer and came out with 40 feet of 1 x 12 pine shelving, a large simi-circular oak stairway and assorted 1 x 2s, 2 x 4s and 1 x 6s.

From the pine he made custom shelves for himself and a friend. He plans to transform the stairs into a coffee table, and the remaining wood will become the formerly hard-to-find "scraps around the shop."

Just try purchasing that much lumber down at your local yard for $3! No, the salvaged lumber isn't brand new or cabinet quality. But if you're looking for material for shelving or furniture, that's a pretty good deal.

ADVERTISING display houses in some larger cities are another good source for scrounging. These firms build booths and signs for trade shows, fairs and permanent exhibits which are installed in airports, hotels and convention halls. The businesses are listed in the Yellow Pages under "Advertising, Display," and they can be good sources of new plywood, fiberglass, plastics and other such materials.

These advertising signs and exhibits are all made from absolutely first-class, brand new materials. This means that the leftovers and scraps from such work are — likewise — new and of superior grade.

You may not get a lot of what you'd call "large pieces," but they'll be plenty big enough for framing pictures, making small desk cubicles and turning into planter boxes.

McKeithan's last junket to a display shop netted him several pieces of birch and mahogany plywood, a few 1 x 2s, and 2 x 2s, assorted pine boards and a couple of plastic signs and painted sections of hardboard from old and junked booths.

Disposal of these odds and ends is generally handled by a janitor who's only too happy to get them off his hands. Another dividend offered by these display shops is the sizable amount of sawdust they produce along with their scraps. The dust makes excellent mulch and compost since it comes almost entirely from hardwoods instead of resinous pines and other softwoods.

But a real scrounger doesn't have to hang around demolition sites or display shops looking for old and new lumber. Cruise the streets immediately ahead of the annual municipal pickup of articles too large for the regular daily or weekly refuse collection.

APPENDIX IV. Visualmaker

The Kodak Ektagraphic Visualmaker consists of an Instamatic x-35 camera, a 3 x 3-inch copy stand, an 8 x 8-inch copy stand, a pistol grip and a wrist strap for the camera. The camera may be used by itself, or it may be locked into one of the copy stands for close up work.

Each stand contains its own built in, prefocused lens, so there is absolutely no focus adjustment for the user to make. Each stand also has a reflector that provides the correct amount of light from the magicube, in order to properly illuminate any subject. Newspaper and magazine materials, photographs, illustrations, graphs, budget figures, charts, even three-dimensional objects may be "snapped" and turned into clear quality color slides (or prints).

The versatility of the visualmaker — a camera for recording library events, a visualmaker for slide show story hours and public relations slide tape work — makes the cost (approximately $140) a very reasonable investment.

APPENDIX V. Ideas

A pot pourri of nifty ideas, some of which require armtwisting, begging par excellence or money!

1. Staff with presstyped pitch on forehead.

2. Streamer from plane or hot air balloon.

3. Placards on buses and taxis.

4. Ads at Drive in Movie theatres.

5. Wildly painted cars, vans or bookmobiles.

6   Bumper stickers.

7. Staff pins with catchy lines instead of names.

8. T shirts

9. Rubber stamps with IMAGINATIVE sayings for book jackets, newspapers.

10. Brightly colored insert for plastic book jackets.

11. Banners over the street.

12. Question kiosks.

13. Ads on entire barn sides, building site walls, apartment buildings. Don't forget that local art departments, community colleges, independent schools could easily make your idea a term project!

14. Placemats at local eateries.

15. Ads on bowling alley score sheets, golf cards.

16. Booths at local carnivals: hook a book, hit the librarian with a wet sponge.

GRATEFUL ACKNOWLEDGMENT
is made to the following:

Ken Kaplowitz, Hopewell, New Jersey, for all library photographs

Mimi Bull and Martin P. Winar for their doodles

Eastman Kodak Company, Rochester, NY, for providing photographs
of their Visualmaker

Congressional Information Service, Inc., Washington, D. C., for
permission to reprint their poster "Ask your Librarian"

The Register and Tribune Syndicate, Inc., Des Moines, Iowa, for
permission to reprint, "Think Scrounge for Materials,"
The Mother Earth News

Fearon-Pitman Publishers, Inc., Belmont, California for permission
to reprint the list of Point of Purchase Advertising
Displays

The Advertising Council, Inc., New York, New York, for graciously
agreeing to respond to requests for their house publication, *Bulletin*

Doyle Dane Bernbach, Inc., for providing Levy's advertising copy

THANKS TO ALL — William, Gregg, Sarah, Susan, Mimi — for making freelance mothering a joyous possibility! And to Jude and Art —
for caring.

ABOUT THE AUTHOR

Ms. Baeckler has served as Librarian for Willard Straight Browsing Library, Ithaca, New York; Head of the Slavic Order Section, Firestone Library, Princeton University; and Head of the Headquarters Library, Mercer County System, Trenton, New Jersey.

Currently, Ms. Baeckler is conducting workshops on popular library topics and has co-authored *GO, PEP and POP! 250 Tested Ideas for Lively Libraries* (U*N*A*B*A*S*H*E*D Librarian, 1976), which is based on experiences at Mercer County Library.

DATE DUE	

Printed by Hermitage Press, Inc., Trenton, New Jersey